Financial Analysis Techniques

Return on Average Total Assets $= \dfrac{\text{net income}}{\text{average total assets}}$

Times Interest Earned $= \dfrac{\text{operating income}}{\text{interest charges}}$

Operating Ratio $= \dfrac{\text{cost of goods sold} + \text{operating expenses}}{\text{net sales}}$

Current (or Working Capital) Ratio $= \dfrac{\text{current assets}}{\text{current liabilities}}$

Quick (Acid) Ratio $= \dfrac{\text{quick assets}}{\text{current liabilities}}$

Inventory Turnover $= \dfrac{\text{cost of goods sold}}{\text{average inventory (at cost)}}$

Accounts Receivable Turnover $= \dfrac{\text{net sales}}{\text{average accounts receivable}}$

Debt Ratio $= \dfrac{\text{total debt}}{\text{total assets}}$

Equity Ratio $= \dfrac{\text{total owner's equity}}{\text{total assets}}$

Debt-to-Equity Ratio $= \dfrac{\text{total debt}}{\text{total owner's equity}}$

Pricing

Selling Price $= \text{cost} + \text{markup}$

$= \text{cost} \times (100\% + \text{markup rate based on cost})$

$= \text{cost} \div (100\% - \text{markup rate based on selling price})$

Conversion of Markup Rates to Another Base

Markup Rate on Cost $= \dfrac{\text{markup rate on selling price}}{100\% - \text{markup rate on selling price}}$

Markup Rate on Selling Price $= \dfrac{\text{markup rate on cost}}{100\% + \text{markup rate on cost}}$

Markdown $= \text{original selling price} - \text{reduced selling price}$

Markdown Rate $= \dfrac{\text{markdown}}{\text{original selling price}}$

Taxes

Property Tax $= \text{assessed value} \times \text{tax rate}$

Sales Tax $= \text{sales price} \times \text{tax rate}$

Insurance

Life Insurance Premium $= \text{rate per \$1000} \times \dfrac{\text{face amount of policy}}{\$1000}$

Operational Mathematics for Business

Second Edition

R. C. PIERCE, JR.

University of Houston

W. J. TEBEAUX

Southwestern Bell

Wadsworth Publishing Company

Belmont, California

A Division of Wadsworth, Inc.

Mathematics Editor: Peter Fairchild
Signing Representative: Ragu Raghaven

© 1983 by Wadsworth, Inc.

Printed in the United States of America

1 2 3 4 5 6 7 8 9 10—87 86 85 84 83

ISBN 0-534-01235-3

Library of Congress Cataloging in Publication Data

Pierce, R. C.
    Operational mathematics for business.

    Includes index.
    1. Business mathematics. I. Tebeaux, W. J.
II. Title.
HF5691.P556   1982   513'.93   82-10977
ISBN 0-534-01235-3

To the principals and interest:
Linda, Karen, Craig
& Beth, Jeffrey, Jason

Second Edition Preface

In 1981 President Ronald Reagan signed the Economic Recovery Tax Act of 1981. The act had significant impact on both business and consumers. This second edition is our effort to address some of the changes wrought by the Tax Act of 1981. We also took the opportunity to enhance the first edition based on suggestions from some of our many users. Briefly stated, the major changes in the second edition are as follows:

1. *Chapter Tests.* We added a comprehensive test at the end of each chapter. This test will allow the student to test his or her knowledge of the material when the problems are presented out of context.

2. *Additional Problems.* We have expanded many problem sets in order to allow greater flexibility in teaching material. Of course, the *solutions* to odd-numbered problems remain as a learning aid. The review exercises contain odd-numbered *answers only*. Problems have also been added to the cumulative reviews for each part.

3. *Negotiable Order of Withdrawal.* The chapter on banking (Chapter 3) has been expanded to reflect some of the new money management devices available to consumers—negotiable order of withdrawal (NOW) accounts.

4. *Cost Recovery.* The Tax Act of 1981 caused significant changes in the process of depreciation. Chapter 9 presents the Accelerated Cost Recovery System (ACRS) created by the tax act; and it relates depreciation and cost recovery for that period when both apply.

5. *Present (and Future) Value of Annuities.* The discussion of amortization (Chapter 14) has been expanded to include the present value of an annuity and the future value of an annuity. Also, we have included new tables relating to annuities.

6. *Securities Purchases.* Chapter 15 (Stocks and Bonds) has been expanded to include the actual mechanics of the transfer of ownership in securities.

7. *Taxes.* Chapter 17 (Taxes) has been expanded to include the fundamentals of income tax. Obviously, income tax is a dynamic field. As such, no text could remain current for long. For this reason, we attempted to provide information on the fundamental process without detailed use of Internal Revenue Service forms. The tax tables are included to familiarize the student with what lies ahead.

8. *Graphing.* The discussion of graphing (Chapter 19) has been expanded to include graphing an equation and circle graphs.

9. *Statistics.* The discussion of statistics (Chapter 20) has been expanded to include measures of variation and the normal distribution in order to give a more complete analysis of data.

10. *Glossary.* The glossary has been greatly expanded. The additional terms will assist the student in completing the first question of each Chapter test. The expanded glossary also enhances the book's value as reference material.

11. *Other Changes.* There are other minor changes made to enhance the "teachability" of the text.

We received many suggestions and comments from users (both students and teachers) of the first edition of *Operational Mathematics for Business*. We are very grateful for these comments and solicit your comments on the second edition. We would also like to express our appreciation to our excellent editors at Wadsworth Publishing Company—Mr. Richard Jones and Mr. Peter Fairchild, and to the following reviewers, whose input was so helpful:

Curtis Askim, Santa Rosa Junior College
Anthony Brunswick, Delaware Technical and Community College
Daniel Fendel, San Francisco State University
Jim Hale, Vance-Granville Community College
Jerry Jones, Aiken Technical College
Ray MacTague, Moorpark College
Cada Parrish, Longwood College
Gary Phillips, Oakton Community College
Thomas Rossi, Broome Community College
David Strong, Prince George's Community College
Richard Tinney, Tidewater Community College
Ron Waite, Blue Mountain Community College
Tom Williams, Seward County Community College

R. C. Pierce, Jr.
William Jene Tebeaux

First Edition Preface

Operational Mathematics for Business is the result of our efforts to provide students with a vehicle for enhancing their mathematical skills and increasing their understanding of many concepts they will encounter in a business career. This text is intended for use in a one-semester course in business mathematics. Although the material exceeds the amount normally covered in a single semester, it is our intention to provide some flexibility in choice of topics and depth of coverage.

The text is divided into five parts. **Part One** provides a complete review of mathematical skills from operations with fractions to solving equations. **Part Two** discusses procedures normally encountered in business, beginning with acquisition of merchandise (purchasing) through measuring the success of the business (via financial statements). **Part Three** presents the mathematical aspects of financial management progressing from simple interest through amortization and sinking funds to corporate financing. **Part Four** discusses topics of benefit to the individual both as a business manager and as a consumer. **Part Five** shows how graphing and statistics are used in decision making and gives an introduction to the metric system.

Several instructional features are used throughout the text to increase its effectiveness as an instructional tool.

1. Each of the five parts begins with an overview that serves to orient the reader to the structure and content of the ensuing chapters. Each part concludes with a cumulative set of review problems designed to reinforce the student's overall comprehension of the concepts presented in that part.

2. Each chapter is preorganized in an introduction. This introduction presents the general learning objectives desired and their relevance to business operations in order to capitalize on the student's pragmatic motivation for learning the material. The chapters are subdivided into sections focusing on one major concept. Each section is accompanied by a set of problems that begin with routine drill exercises and progressively increase in difficulty. Each chapter concludes with a comprehensive set of review problems.

3. The text has numerous examples written in a straightforward format: each example first states the problem, then presents a detailed solution. Examples are presented for every concept discussed.

4. The marginal notation of key factors and formulas provides for ready reference and quick location of items within a chapter.

5. Answers to selected problems are normally given to allow students to verify the accuracy of their work. If the student's answer does not agree with that given in the text, the answer is of little benefit in helping the student determine his mistake. Hence, we have included *worked-out solutions* deriving the answers to odd-numbered problems in each section.

6. A glossary of major mathematical and business terms is included.

7. A list of key formulas used in the major concepts requiring mathematical computations is included. This list provides a ready reference for use during the course and a future business career.

Most of us really do not know what a book is like until it has been used in class and we get feedback on how it works. That is why later editions of texts are generally better learning and teaching tools than are earlier editions.

A first edition can never be a third edition. But it can come close if we get—and respond to—enough advance help from experienced teachers. The following reviewers have made an invaluable contribution to the reliability and teachability of this text:

William Babcock, Motlow State Community College
Barry J. Bomboy, J. Sargeant Reynolds Community College
Mary B. Fuller, St. Louis Community College at Forest Park
Bernard Karne, Laney College
John Kroencke, Victor Valley College
Gwendolyn Loftis, Oscar Rose Junior College
Frank Martin, Chattanooga State Technical Community College
Frank O. McDaniels, Delaware County Community College
Alta Givens Mears, Oscar Rose Community College
Jerry W. Miller, College of DuPage
Gena Ousley, Chaffey College
S. Rondfong, Youngstown State University
Helen Schoon, Madison Area Technical College
William Scott, Ocean County College

We would also like to thank the *Wall Street Journal*; Frank D. Kleinworth III of Tools, Inc.; and Sidney Dean of South Main Bank for their contributions to the text. Our very special thanks go to Linda B. Pierce; Wesley J. Knebel, CLU of Connecticut Mutual Life Insurance Company, and Bob Hataway of State Farm Insurance Company for their technical assistance in manuscript content. The manuscript would not have been possible without the expert typing of Jan Want. Last, but certainly not least, our deepest appreciation to Richard Jones, Mathematics Editor, Wadsworth Publishing Company, for his continuing support during the manuscript preparation.

R. C. Pierce, Jr.
William Jene Tebeaux

Contents